Water Cycle and Weather

by Harrison James

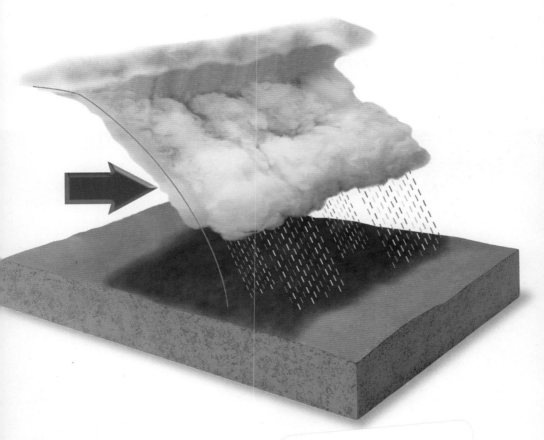

D1555660

PEARSON

Scott
Foresman

Where is Earth's water?

Earth—The Water Planet

Water is found all over Earth. Bodies of water can be used to get from one place to another. Nearly $\frac{3}{4}$ of the surface of Earth is covered with water. Millions of organisms live in water. These organisms get their food from water. People can use these organisms for food.

Water can be a liquid, solid, or gas. At 0°C, water freezes into ice, which is a solid. Ice melts into liquid water at this temperature. At 100°C, water becomes water vapor, which is a gas.

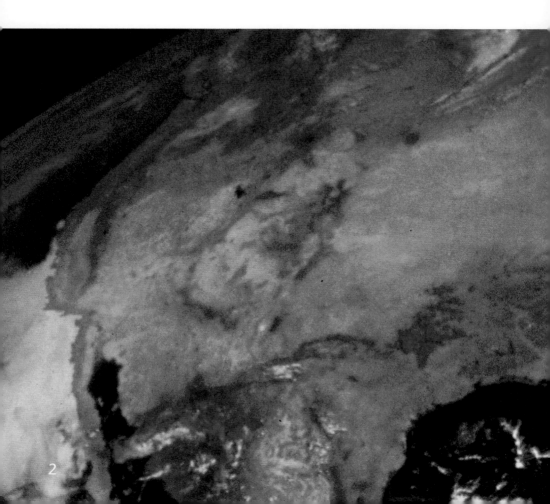

Some water near Earth's surface is water vapor. This is mostly water that is found in the atmosphere. But the oceans and seas make up more than $\frac{97}{100}$ of the water found on Earth. Almost all of the rest is frozen in glaciers and polar ice caps. Lakes and rivers make up less than $\frac{1}{100}$ of the water on Earth.

All the oceans of the world are connected. They make up one huge body of salty water. The ocean is divided into sections. Each section is given a name. Look at the chart to see the name and the size of each section.

Approximate Areas of the Oceans of the World					
Ocean	Pacific	Atlantic	Indian	Southern	Arctic
Area (km²)	165 million	82 million	73 million	20 million	14 million

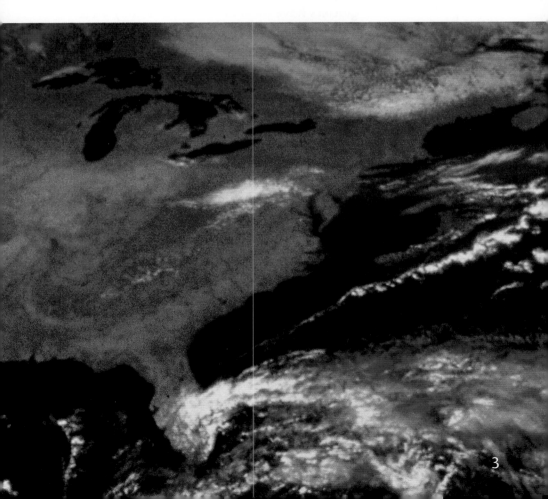

Salty Water

Ocean water tastes different from our drinking water. Ocean water is very salty. In fact, it is so salty that it is not good to drink. The human body cannot use water that is as salty as the ocean.

Water is made of hydrogen and oxygen. Rivers have dissolved salt and minerals in them. They carry these dissolved materials to the ocean. Ocean water is water mixed with many dissolved solids. Much of the salt in ocean water comes from these dissolved solids. Most of the salt in the ocean is the same salt you use on food. In fact, most of our table salt comes from the ocean.

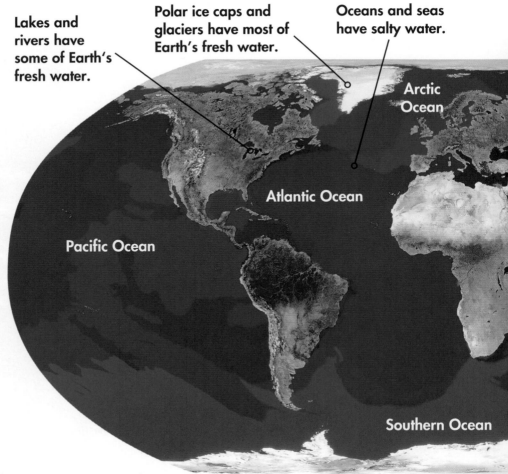

Lakes and rivers have some of Earth's fresh water.

Polar ice caps and glaciers have most of Earth's fresh water.

Oceans and seas have salty water.

Arctic Ocean

Atlantic Ocean

Pacific Ocean

Southern Ocean

Differences in Saltiness

Not all water at the surface of the ocean has the same amount of salt. In warm, dry places, water from the ocean quickly moves into the air as water vapor. Salt does not move into the air. The ocean water that's left is even saltier.

The ocean water around the North and South Poles is less salty. Water does not become water vapor as quickly in cold places as it does in warm places. There is also less salt in areas where a lot of fresh water mixes with ocean water. The fresh water can come from rivers, melting ice, and heavy rain.

Most water on Earth is salty ocean water. Some fresh water is in lakes, rivers, and streams. Much of Earth's fresh water is frozen in glaciers and polar ice caps.

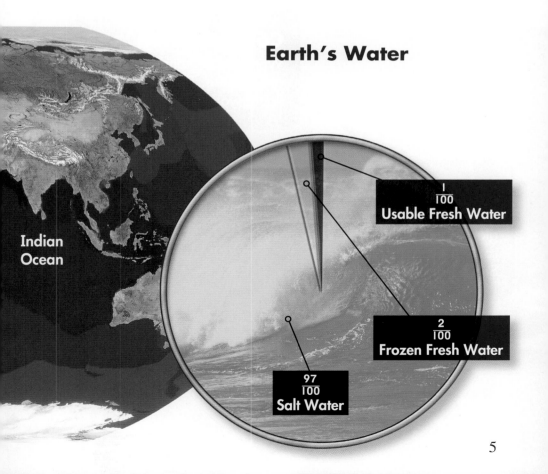

Earth's Water

Indian
Ocean

$\frac{1}{100}$
Usable Fresh Water

$\frac{2}{100}$
Frozen Fresh Water

$\frac{97}{100}$
Salt Water

5

How do water and air affect weather?

How Water Is Recycled

Water moves from the surface of Earth into the atmosphere and back again. This is the water cycle. After it rains, some water will flow into lakes, rivers, or the ocean. The rest will go into the air. The particles that make up water are always moving. Light from the Sun heats them and makes them move faster. The particles become a gas called water vapor. **Evaporation** is liquid water changing into water vapor.

Condensation

Water vapor condenses in the atmosphere. These tiny droplets of liquid water form clouds and fog.

Evaporation

Water is stored in lakes, oceans, glaciers, marshes, soil, and spaces in rock. It evaporates in the Sun's warmth.

Water vapor turns to liquid when the temperature is low. **Condensation** is water vapor becoming liquid when it cools.

Clouds are made of tiny drops of water or crystals of ice. These drops and crystals join together until they are so heavy that gravity pulls them downward to Earth's surface. **Precipitation** is water in any form that falls to Earth.

Temperature, the movement of air, and the amount of water vapor in the air affect the water cycle. Land features, such as mountains, also have an effect. Clouds form when wind blows moist air up one side of a mountain. More precipitation will fall on that side of the mountain. Water moves through the water cycle. The total amount of water on Earth does not change.

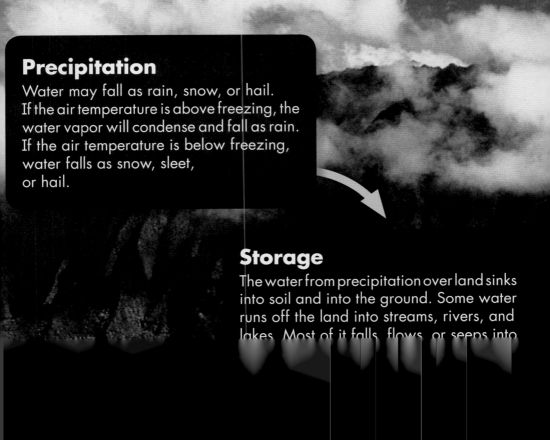

Precipitation
Water may fall as rain, snow, or hail. If the air temperature is above freezing, the water vapor will condense and fall as rain. If the air temperature is below freezing, water falls as snow, sleet, or hail.

Storage
The water from precipitation over land sinks into soil and into the ground. Some water runs off the land into streams, rivers, and lakes. Most of it falls, flows, or seeps into

The Earth's Atmosphere

The atmosphere is the blanket of air around Earth. Air has mass. It takes up space. Air is made of invisible gases. Nitrogen makes up nearly $\frac{4}{5}$ of the atmosphere. The rest is mostly oxygen, with some carbon dioxide gas. The part of the atmosphere that is closest to Earth's surface has water vapor. Air over a desert has less water vapor than air over an ocean.

Air pressure is the pushing force of air. Air pushes in all directions with the same amount of force. Air pushing up is balanced by air pushing down.

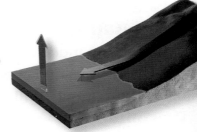

A land breeze moves from land to the sea. At night, the cool air over land sinks and moves toward the water.

Air Pressure

Temperature can change air pressure. The particles of warm air near the surface of Earth move quickly. The air rises and then pushes down with less pressure. This makes an area of low pressure. If the air near the surface of Earth becomes cool, its particles will move slowly. This dense air will sink.

Wind is air moving from an area of high pressure to an area of low pressure. Wind is named for the direction from which it comes. A north wind comes from the north and moves south.

A sea breeze moves from the sea to land. During the day, the warm air over land rises. The air over the water moves toward the land.

As you go even higher, air pressure is even lower.

Higher in the atmosphere, the particles in the air move farther apart. Air pressure is lower.

Air particles are close together at Earth's surface. Closely packed particles have greater pressure than loosely packed particles.

What are air masses?

Air Masses

An air mass is a vast body of air with almost the same temperature and humidity. **Humidity** is the amount of water vapor in the air. Most weather comes from how air masses move and interact. Air masses are heated or cooled by the land or water over which they form. This can take several days, or even weeks. A cool or cold air mass forms over polar areas. A warm or hot air mass forms over tropical areas.

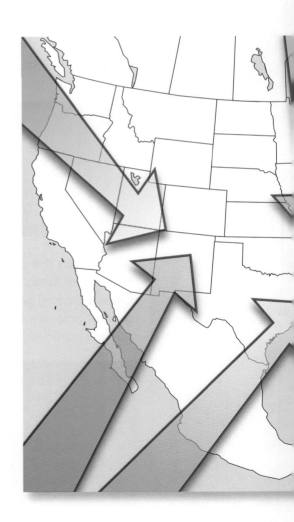

An air mass has water vapor in it. This water vapor is water that has evaporated from the land or body of water below the air mass. An air mass that forms over water has more humidity than one that forms over land. An air mass that forms over a warm ocean will most likely be warm and humid. An air mass that forms over a cool ocean will be cool and humid.

Temperature and humidity move with air masses. Scientists follow the movement of air masses to predict the weather. They also study where and how air masses will meet. Weather is how air, water, and temperature interact.

In the United States, air masses from the south bring warmer weather than those from the north.

When Air Masses Meet: Cold Front

Over North America, air masses usually move from west to east. Air masses that have different temperatures and humidity can meet. The air masses do not mix. A **front** is the area where two different air masses meet.

A cold front comes from a cold air mass meeting a slower moving warm air mass. Cold air is denser than warm air. The dense, cold air moves below the warm air. The warm air becomes cooler as it is pushed up. Water vapor in the cooling air forms clouds.

Cold fronts can cause strong winds and heavy, brief precipitation. Cold fronts move quickly. After they pass, the weather is usually cooler and fair.

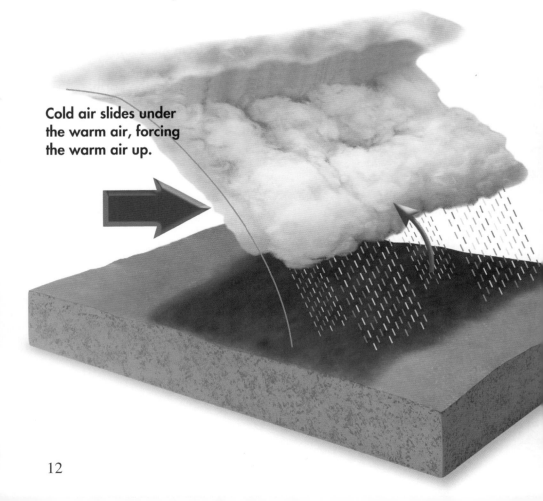

Cold air slides under the warm air, forcing the warm air up.

When Air Masses Meet: Warm Front

A warm front forms when a warm air mass meets a slower moving cold air mass. The warm air is less dense than the cold air. The warm air rises above the cold air and becomes cooler. Water vapor in the air forms clouds.

Warm fronts move more slowly than cold fronts. They can affect weather over a larger area for a longer period of time. Warm fronts bring long-lasting precipitation. They often bring higher temperatures.

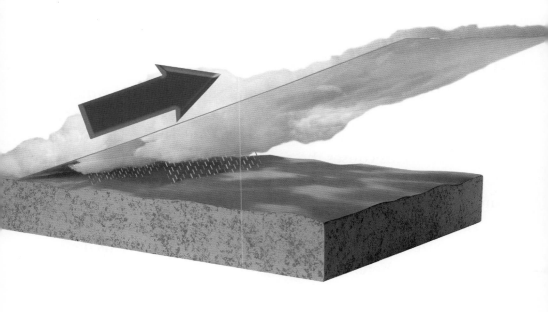

A warm air mass slowly rises over a cold air mass. Warm fronts may last for a long time.

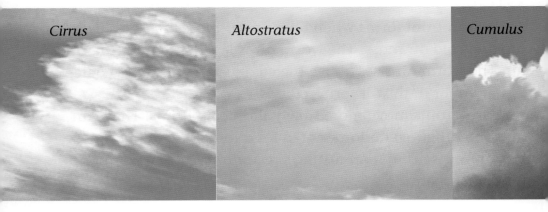

Cirrus   *Altostratus*   *Cumulus*

Clouds

Clouds begin to take shape as the Sun warms the water in oceans, rivers, lakes, and the ground. The warm water evaporates and water vapor enters the air. This air is warmed by the Sun. This causes the air to rise and cool. The water vapor forms water drops and ice crystals. These drops and crystals are clouds.

There are many kinds of clouds. They can have different shapes, sizes, and colors. The kind of cloud that forms depends on the atmosphere.

Cumulonimbus

Stratus

Ten names are used to describe most clouds. The names are combinations of three main types of clouds. The main types of clouds are cumulus, stratus, and cirrus. Adding *alto* to a cloud's name means the cloud is very high. *Nimbo* means a cloud will bring rain.

Cumulus clouds are thick, white, and puffy. They look like pieces of cotton. You see them when the weather is good. They may be high in the sky. Stratus clouds form flat layers. They are close to Earth's surface. Cirrus clouds are feathery. They form high in the atmosphere when water vapor turns to ice crystals.

How do we measure and predict weather?

Measuring Weather

Temperature, air pressure, and water affect weather. Ocean currents move warm water to cold lands. They also move cold water to warm lands. Areas near water may have milder temperatures than areas farther away.

A **meteorologist** is a scientist who studies weather conditions. Meteorologists study temperature, water, and air movement. They get information from weather observation stations.

A thermometer measures air temperature. A **barometer** measures air pressure. Air pressure is often measured in millibars (mb).

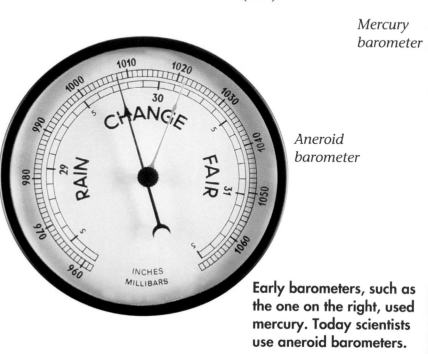

Mercury barometer

Aneroid barometer

Early barometers, such as the one on the right, used mercury. Today scientists use aneroid barometers.

Air Pressure and Weather Conditions

You can tell some things about air pressure by looking outside. Weather is often damp and cloudy when air pressure is low. High air pressure often comes with dry and clear weather.

An **anemometer** measures wind speed. It has three or four cups on top. The cups spin in the wind. As the wind blows harder, the cups spin faster. A **wind vane** shows the direction from which wind is blowing. The arrow on the wind vane points into the wind.

A rain gauge measures how much rain has fallen. A hygrometer measures humidity.

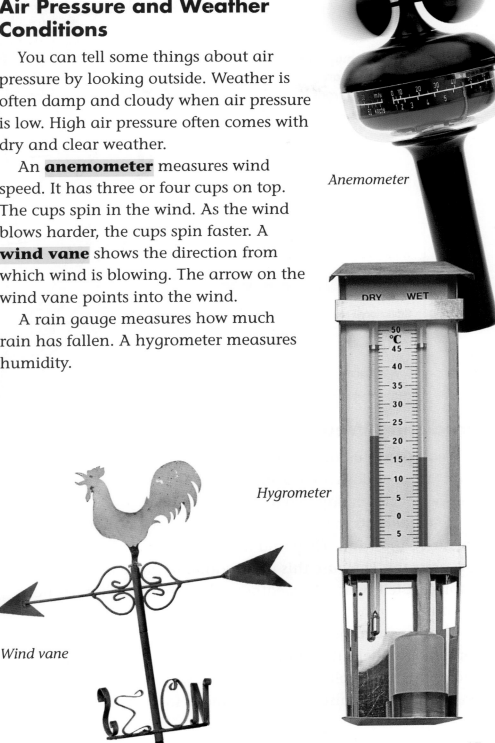

Anemometer

Hygrometer

Wind vane

A weather map shows
where fronts are.
A stationary front is
not moving.

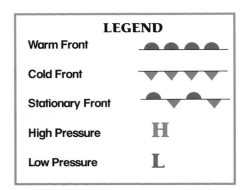

LEGEND

Warm Front	●●●●
Cold Front	▼▼▼▼
Stationary Front	●▼●▼
High Pressure	**H**
Low Pressure	**L**

Predicting Weather

Weather in the same place is usually similar from year to year. Summer days are warmer than winter days. Figuring out the weather from day to day is not as easy.

Meteorologists measure temperature, precipitation, air pressure, and wind. They find fronts and areas of high and low pressure. They use this information to make a forecast. A forecast tells what the weather will probably be for the next few days.

Weather radar gives information that is used to make computer models. Radar pictures show how the atmosphere is changing. Meteorologists can find out where rain has fallen. This information also helps them make forecasts.

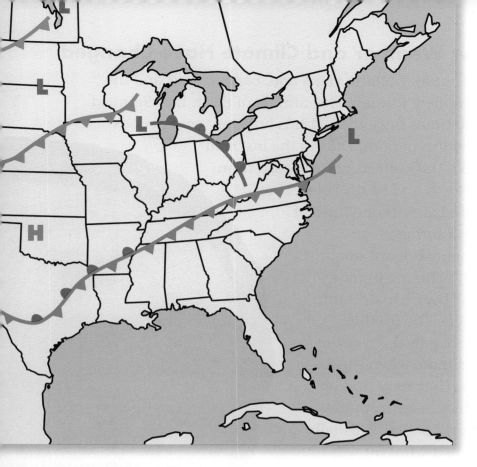

Tracking Weather

Measurements and information from weather radar and satellites are put into maps and charts. Meteorologists use this to predict weather. Charts can record daily weather conditions.

Reading Weather Maps

A weather map uses symbols to show fronts and weather conditions. A legend, or key, explains what everything means. The letters H and L show areas of high and low pressure. Triangles on lines mean cold fronts. Half circles mean warm fronts.

How Weather and Climate Have Changed

About four billion years ago, Earth cooled and the atmosphere formed. The climate of Earth has changed many times since then. It has had very cold periods and warm periods. During the last cold period, thick sheets of ice spread from the North and South Poles. They covered almost one-third of Earth's surface.

Scientists learn about Earth's climate in many ways. They can drill into glaciers. The ice they remove tells them about the climate when the ice froze. They may find air bubbles in ice from the last cold period. This tells scientists what air was like when it was trapped.

Tree rings can tell scientists about the climate when the tree was growing. You can see rings in a cut tree trunk. Each ring in a tree trunk shows the growth that took place in one year. A wide ring means there were good growing conditions that year.

Earth's crust can also give scientists information about past climates. Scientists can estimate when each layer of the crust was formed. Coal found in the crust means that layer formed during a warm climate. Coal forms from bodies of organisms that lived long ago in warm climates.

At Present

Earth's climate has experienced cycles in the last two and a half million years. A warm period is followed by a cold period. Then another warm period takes over. We are in a warm period now. The last cold period ended about ten thousand years ago. Earth's climate and temperature change slowly during these cycles. Some scientists worry that people are causing Earth's temperature to change more quickly than it would on its own. They are concerned that these man-made changes are harmful.

In the Future

Burning fossil fuels adds carbon dioxide and other pollutants to the atmosphere. There are "greenhouse gases" in our atmosphere. Some of these are water vapor and carbon dioxide. In the right amount, greenhouse gases help keep Earth warm. Too many greenhouse gases increase the temperature of Earth. Climates may change if Earth's temperature rises even a few degrees. Part of the polar ice caps could melt. This could add water to oceans. This could lead to flooding.

Scientists and world leaders are looking for ways to replace fossil fuels with cleaner energy. Using cleaner energy in smaller amounts will be better for Earth. These efforts show how important it is to protect Earth.

Scientists can study blocks of ice from glaciers to learn about climates.

Glossary

anemometer   a tool that measures wind speed

barometer   a tool that measures air pressure

condensation   water vapor changing into liquid

evaporation   liquid water changing into water vapor

front   the area where two air masses meet

humidity   the amount of water vapor in the air

meteorologist   a scientist who studies weather conditions

precipitation   water in any form that falls to Earth

wind vane   a tool that shows wind direction